My Adoption Book

Written by Sharon Guenther

Illustrated by Heather Goodfallow

Copyright © 2011 by Sharon Guenther

First Edition –May 2011

ISBN
978-1-77067-556-8 (Paperback)
978-1-77067-557-5 (eBook)

All rights reserved.

No part of this publication may be reproduced in any form, or by any means, electronic or mechanical, including photocopying, recording, or any information browsing, storage, or retrieval system, without permission in writing from the publisher.

Published by:

FriesenPress
Suite 300 – 852 Fort Street
Victoria, BC, Canada V8W 1H8

www.friesenpress.com

Distributed to the trade by The Ingram Book Company

Table of Contents

Author's Note 1

Information 3

Other Information 7

Photos and Momentos 9

Year One 11

Other One Year Information 13

One Year Photos and Momentos 15

Year Two 17

Other Two Year Information 19

Two Year Photos and Momentos 21

Year Three 23

Other Three Year Information 25

Three Year Photos and Momentos 27

Year Four 29

Other Year Four Information 31

Year Four Photos and Momentos 33

Information For Future Years 35

Future Years Photos

and Momentos 37

My Adoption Book

Have you ever adopted an animal and wondered about the best way to care for them? Do you wish you had an insight into "communicating" with your new pet?

Well, this book was created to help people with their pets. Here you will find a questionnaire that contains everything from birthdays (or adoption days) to where your pet likes to sleep. Once completed, you can use it to provide useful information in the event that your pet is lost, stolen or must be given away. It is also useful for anyone who takes care of your pet or you can use it as a baby book for your pet!

This book makes a great gift to new "parents". From the AKC breeds to the mixed breed at the shelter, they all have stories to be told for their optimum care and comfort.

A portion of the proceeds from the sale of this book will go to the ASPCA.

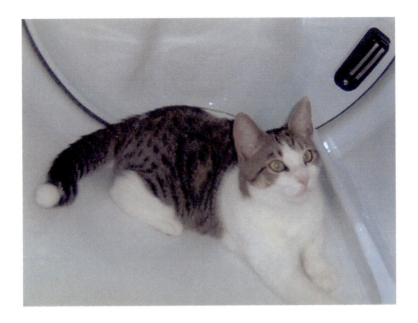

This book is dedicated
to Warlock, my beloved wolf.

My Adoption Book

My Adoption Book

My Adoption Book

My Adoption Book

My Adoption Book

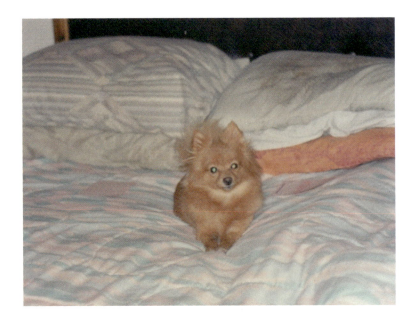

My Adoption Book

My Adoption Book

My Adoption Book

My Adoption Book

Author's Note

This book came about in a unique way.

I had just broken up with my boyfriend and I had no place that I could keep my wolf. So, after finding a good home for him, I started thinking. How were they going to know his favorite treat or where he liked to be scratched? Would they know that he liked only rawhide bones?

So I sat down and completed a pamphlet for the new owners.

And that is how this book came to be. Can you imagine if all pets had an adoption book that came with them? It would take the guesswork out of things like what food to buy or when yearly shots were due.

If you are a new "parent" buying this book or if you are buying it for a friend let me thank you. I hope you have as much fun with this book as I did in creating it.

Congratulations on your new addition!

My Adoption Book

Information

My name is _____

I am   male   female

I am a _____

My mother is a _____

Her name is _____

My father is a _____

His name is _____

I was born/adopted on _____

I was born, or found at _____

I had _____ brothers and _____ sisters.

I weigh _____

My color is _____

My eyes are _____

My Adoption Book

I have papers (AKC, UKC, etc.) _____

I had my first shots on_____

I got my shots at_____

I was de-wormed on _____

I was de-wormed at_____

I opened my eyes on_____

I have had the following done (clip tails or ears, remove

claws, etc.)_____

I have been spayed/ neutered   yes   no

I have the following scars or identifying marks

_____

I have the following limitations or defect

_____

My medical records are at

_____

My Adoption Book

I am potty-trained   yes   no

When I have to potty I will tell you by
_____

I get car sick   yes   no

I am leash trained   yes   no

I can be disciplined by_____

I was trained to_____

I don't like_____

I get along with children   yes   no

I get along with other animals   yes   no

I weigh _____

I have been known to bite or scratch when
_____

I love the following people food
_____

My favorite pet food is
_____

I eat_____times a day. AM PM

For treats I like_____

My favorite toy is_____

My favorite trick is_____

My favorite game is _____

I like it when you (scratch my tummy, throw a ball, etc.)
_____

I like to sleep (on the floor, in the bed, etc.)
_____

Other Information

Other Information

Photos and Momentos

My Adoption Book

Year One

I am now_____ years old and weigh_____

I got my shots on_____

I got my shots at _____

We celebrated my birthday by
_____

For my birthday I got_____

I can do the following tricks
_____
_____
_____

My favorite treats are _____

My favorite food is _____

I really like it when _____

I don't like it when _____

My Adoption Book

Other One Year Information

My Adoption Book

One Year Photos and Momentos

My Adoption Book

Year Two

I am now_____ years old and weigh_____

I got my shots on_____

I got my shots at _____

We celebrated my birthday by

_____

_____

_____

For my birthday I got_____

I can do the following tricks

_____

My favorite treats are_____

My favorite food is_____

I really like it when _____

I don't like it when _____

17

Other Two Year Information

My Adoption Book

Two Year Photos and Momentos

My Adoption Book

Year Three

I am now_____ years old and weigh_____

I got my shots on_____

I got my shots at _____

We celebrated my birthday by

_____

_____

_____

For my birthday I got_____

I can do the following tricks

_____

My favorite treats are_____

My favorite food is_____

I really like it when _____

I don't like it when _____

My Adoption Book

Other Three Year Information

My Adoption Book

Three Year Photos and Momentos

My Adoption Book

Year Four

I am now_____years old and weigh_____

I got my shots on_____

I got my shots at _____

We celebrated my birthday by
_____
_____
_____

For my birthday I got_____

I can do the following tricks
_____

My favorite treats are_____

My favorite food is_____

I really like it when _____

I don't like it when _____

My Adoption Book

Other Year Four Information

My Adoption Book

Year Four Photos and Momentos

Information For Future Years

My Adoption Book

Future Years Photos and Momentos